POWER OF NEGOTIATING

Strategies for Success

by
Mike R. Stark

Dick,

May the Power of Negotiating be with you!

Mike

TRIMARK
PUBLISHING

Page Composition: Trimark Publishing
Cover: Network Graphics
Editor: Criscadian - Editorial Services

ISBN 0-9649453-0-4

Library of Congress Catalog Card Number: 95-90945

Printing 1 2 3 4 5 6 7 8 9 10

DEDICATION

*This book is dedicated to my parents,
who became the first "victims" of my
subconscious negotiation practices,
and to my wife, Candie, who taught me
that not everything remains negotiable
once you say "I do."*

TABLE OF CONTENTS

page

PREFACE

This book is designed for professionals who want to enhance their success in business and for everyone who would like to better his or her odds in everyday negotiations.

Having read an abundance of literature about negotiation, I felt that people interested in learning about different styles of negotiations usually don't want to waste a lot of time reading through pages of redundance. It was my goal to compose a book that addresses all important techniques and lists relevant "do's and don'ts" in a compact, no-fluff way that is easy to read and apply. Each chapter contains bottom-line information which can be tested immediately in real life situations.

To maximize the benefit from this book, I strongly recommend the reader practice all described negotiation techniques in every possible way. Negotiate the rate for your hotel room, the price for a car, and your next pay raise. This will not only help you gain experience and become more successful in your negotiations, but it will also prove to be quite fun.

I

WHAT IS NEGOTIATION?

Every year people graduate from the finest colleges in the country. They have learned the latest technologies in their particular fields, and feel prepared to go out into the business world, eager to apply their knowledge to real life situations. However, there is one factor missing: Nobody taught them anything about negotiating.

It is, of course, crucial to know how to gather data and to prepare a knockout presentation, but it is just as important to close the deal. To do that you must know how to deal with other people and how to negotiate. It's important to your company when dealing with other businesses, vendors, and clients, and to you when discussing a raise, presenting a complaint to the customer service department, or buying a new car.

You negotiate throughout your life. You should realize that almost everything you would like to have is currently owned by someone else. It is therefore necessary to find socially acceptable ways to obtain these things. That's where negotiation techniques come in. The negotiation tactics I advocate in this book are not sneaky tricks, that a con artist would use, they are ethical methods of persuasion, understanding, and compromise.

Even if you decide not to actively use any these tactics in your negotiations, knowing about them will still be of enormous value to you because others will be using them on you.

II

THE TEN COMMANDMENTS OF NEGOTIATING

1.   Find a way to give the other party what they want.

2.   There are always predictable responses in any given negotiation. To gain the leading edge, you will have to learn how to predict them. This will be easier in some cases than in others, but the responses will always remain quite predictable.

Example

Suppose you are shopping for a used car. You see an ad in the paper advertising the car you want for $8,000, which happens to be below the car's "blue book" value. You make an appointment to look at the vehicle. You are eager to make an offer, although you are prepared to pay the asking price for it, you want to practice your negotiation skills by making a "low-ball" offer:

---

6 / THE POWER OF NEGOTIATING

"Okay, I am willing to pay $6,000 for this car." You expect the seller to get angry about this ridiculously low offer. Then you will strategically work your way up, and will finally reach an agreement around the $7,500 mark, saving you $500.

To your surprise the seller doesn't get angry. He rubs his chin and says that, considering he really needs to sell the car, he will accept your offer of $6,000.

What would your response be in this situation? At first you would probably feel that today was your lucky day; you would be very proud of your bargain buy. On the way home, however, you might get the feeling that you could have done better! Your low offer was accepted right away and you get the feeling that you could offered even less, regardless of the actual price.

Or you might think, "There has to be something wrong with this car!" Both of these after-thoughts are perfectly predictable responses.

3. Find out the other party's motivation. How eager are they to sell or buy? Look for signs they are trying to rush to a solution. If so, they will be more willing to make concessions and to meet more of your demands.

4. Never accept the first offer! By accepting the first offer someone makes, you are forfeiting any possible advantage through negotiating.

5. People react differently to certain situations. You therefore should learn when and how to adapt other negotiation styles. This will be covered in more detail in chapter X of this book.

6. It is not only the spoken word that effects the negotiation process. Learn how to correctly interpret body language signals, and how to send the right signals yourself. Chapter XI takes an in depth look at how to interpret body language, and how to send non-verbal signals when negotiating.

7. Help bring the discussion back to the subject. Some people have a tendency to slide away from the topic, especially if they feel uncomfortable discussing it.

    It is a common tactic to "break the ice" during an initial meeting by talking about something personal and unrelated to the actual issue. This is perfectly fine and will help you establish rapport. After you have established the necessary conversation base, you should forge ahead and steer the discussion straight to the main topic.

8. Know your final price. If you are negotiating the purchase of goods or services, you should know the maximum price you are willing to pay, (or the lowest price you are willing to accept, if you are on the seller's side) prior to entering the negotiations.

    Put a lot of thought into determining your top or bottom figures, and try to stick to them, but don't let a deal fall apart because of a nominal difference.

9. Adopt a laissez faire attitude. Negotiations always favor the party who seems to care least about the transaction. If you show you are extremely eager to close the deal, the price will stay high (or low) and the terms won't be as favorable to you as they could have been.

    Don't limit your options. There is nothing like competition to increase interest. As a seller you should stress that several other buyers have been inquiring about your product. As a buyer, make it clear that you will compare product, price, and terms with other sellers.

10. Success can only be achieved by realizing that negotiating is a two-way street. Negotiating means working <u>with</u> the other party to reach mutually beneficial and satisfactory results.

III

WIN-WIN NEGOTIATIONS

There are three possible outcomes in any negotiation:

1. One party manages to walk away with a "steal," and the other party gets the "raw end of the stick." This is commonly known as a win-lose situation.

    While this outcome initially may seem perfectly acceptable to the winner, it might prove to have been an unsuccessful conclusion after all. The loser will definitely never again do business with the winner. Every bus-iness owner knows the importance of repeat business.

2. Sometimes both parties refuse to compromise and soon find themselves in a hopeless stalemate. This is a lose-lose situation that neither party wanted.

3. The third possibility is the win-win outcome. If both parties are willing to make some concessions, and still feel good about the results of these negotiations, a win-win solution has been reached. It is not necessary for both parties to compromise equally.

That's where it is important to know how to negotiate. There is absolutely nothing wrong with securing a
more favorable result during a negotiation process. As
long as both parties walk away satisfied, a win-win
outcome has been achieved — and the foundation for
future business relations has been laid.

How to Aim for Win-Win Solutions

1. Never narrow down a negotiation to only one issue.
   There is always more than one issue that can become a
   vital part in the negotiation process.

Example

A sports management company wanted to take tennis star
Boris Becker under contract. The negotiations were about
to end because Boris asked for $80,000 advance money,
which the management company did not want to pay. All
other contractual issues were already agreed upon. This
issue was the only one left to address.

The best way (and often the only way) to escape
from such a stalemate would be to re-open certain issues,
such as contract duration, exclusivity, Boris' time involvement, annual fees, etc.

2. People usually don't want the same things. All of us see things in our own, unique perspective. Issues that are very important for me, might be of much less importance for someone else.

    In the movie *Dead Poet Society,* Robin Williams asked all of his students to climb up on his desk to see their worlds from that new perspective.

    Applied to negotiating, this example shows us that two people can look at the same thing and yet describe it differently.

3. Never assume that the other parties want exactly the same as you. It is often possible to give the other parties what they want and still accomplish your negotiation goals.

Example

An applicant responded to a classified ad for the position of executive secretary in my company. The interview went well, and I decided to hire her. She turned out to be an excellent employee, but she did not seem to be really happy at her job. Since our positive work environment could not have been responsible for that, I assumed that she might be dissatisfied with her salary. I gave her a raise. She was definitely grateful for her pay increase, but something still kept her from being completely satisfied with her job.

Eventually, I was approached by one of her co-workers, who told me that the reason she was upset had nothing to do with her income. She was disappointed that the job title on her business cards read, "Secretary" instead of "Executive Secretary." Her title was much more important to her than the raise she received.

That day I ordered a new set of business cards for her, listing her job title as "Executive Secretary." What a small price to pay to maintain job satisfaction.

Learn about the other person in a negotiation. Find out what you must give to your opponent in order to get exactly what you want. View the facts from your perspective and your counterpart's. When you can foresee the other party's responses, you will be one step ahead in the game. Putting yourself in your counterpart's shoes can help you find satisfactory solutions you otherwise might never have thought of.

The worst position to be in during a negotiation is facing indifference. It is easier to deal with total objection than with disinterest. When faced with indifference, you don't know what your counterpart's problems and viewpoints are. You will find it very difficult to reach an agreement.

A marriage counselor once told me that he found it much easier to help couples overcome their problems when they actually said they hated each other, than when they showed total indifference toward each other.

4.   Don't lose focus of what a win-win solution really is! Every good thing can be stretched to such an extreme that it becomes a bad thing.

In a negotiation training session I conducted, I witnessed how one group tried so hard to compromise with their counterparts, that they created a win-lose situation in which they were the losers. Trying to reach a win-win solution has it's limits.

Don't feed your opponent concessions just to set the stage for a fair, win-win outcome. The other party probably will take full advantage of you.

IV

THE FIVE STAGES OF EACH NEGOTIATION

1. Assess the Actual Problem

Before you start to negotiate, you have to define the problem. Be prepared to learn that the actual problem is quite different from what it first appeared to be. Each party's individual perception of a problem may distort the factual parameters.

Example

Bob Smith is in his boss' office to ask for a raise that he feels is long overdue. His performance has been excellent. His boss, Sue Campbell, does not dispute Bob's outstanding performance and loyalty to the company, but Bob is already the highest paid research analyst on staff. Giving him a raise would open the legendary can of worms among his peers, who will also expect raises.

At first it appears to be a typical gridlock situation: Bob wants a raise, but Sue can't give him one.

An objective analysis of this situation will find important, common denominators. The win-win solution to aim for would be to find a way to give Bob the raise without exceeding the company's standard salary ranges.

Sue decided to create a new position of Assistant Research Director to accommodate Bob's request for a raise. At the same time, she avoids a flood of raise requests from all the other research analysts.

2. The Other Party's Goal

Sometimes you will find your counterpart's demands fairly easy to meet.

Example

Several years ago I managed a gymnastics club in Southern California. I happened to be out of the country on vacation, when a nine-year-old girl fell off the uneven bars, suffering a complicated break of her elbow. Her coach and the entire board of directors were in shock about this incident. They were expecting a lawsuit to be filed against them by the girl's parents, asking for more money than the corporation was able to pay.

Upon my return I was briefed on what happened. It was then my responsibility to deal with the problem. The directors were willing to pay up to $50,000 through their insurance, but wanted to avoid legal action at all cost.

I contacted the child's family, and inquired how the child was recuperating. "What we can do to help," I asked. To my surprise, I found that this was the first time anybody had asked the parents this simple question.

"Well," the mother said, "our health insurance will cover all medical expenses. We are, however, concerned that Lisa might have gotten discouraged through her accident and might lose interest in gymnastics. If you could help her overcome any fear she might develop, we would really appreciate it."

Two days later I personally dropped off an autographed Mary Lou Retton poster along with a giant get-well card signed by her teammates. In addition, I gave her a gymnastics video of the recent gymnastics world championships to keep her interested.

All directors congratulated me for my incredibly successful negotiation results. What they did not know was, all I did was ask the other party what it is they wanted.

Unfortunately, it is not always that easy to find out what the other party's wants and expectations are. Sometimes you have to search for pieces of information like a detective. When doing so, make sure you don't just focus on the actual answers you are getting. A great portion of viable information is often hidden in body language and certain phrases. (See Chapters IX and XI.)

3. What Are You Able to Do?

By letting the other party know what you are willing and able to do, you help to establish how far everyone is from reaching an agreement. Don't be disappointed if you find yourself in a situation where there is absolutely no way you can give the other party what they want.

You cannot expect all of your negotiations to be successful, but this will help you to know exactly where everyone stands on certain issues. You will avoid wasting time and energy on issues that will eventually end up getting stuck in permanent gridlock.

4. Gather More Information

One of the key elements of successful negotiating is gathering information about the other side. The more you know about your counterpart, the better your chance of success will be. Typically, the party with the most information will be in control. The enormous advantage of being in control in a negotiation cannot be stressed enough. However, studies show that in only one out of ten times does a negotiating party gather sufficient information about the other side.

You should be aware of this when you enter your next negotiation. You can easily use it to your advantage. If you follow the rules and prepare yourself by gathering information, you will likely be able to obtain control in your negotiations because nine out of ten times your opponents will have failed to do the same.

A. How do You Obtain Information?

The first step in our quest for information can be achieved by simply using the familiar, *"Who? What? When? Where? Why?"* Don't be afraid to ask! You will be surprised how much information people are willing to disclose voluntarily. It is just a matter of asking the right questions.

The best way of probing for information is by asking more open-ended questions. Open-ended questions are questions that cannot be answered with "Yes" or "No," but require much more detailed answers. Very often you can find valuable information about somebody's actual needs and wants by asking open-ended questions. It can also generate information about the counterpart's personality style.

Ten hints to asking good and effective questions:

♦ Prepare a plan for questioning.

♦ Ask only relevant questions.

♦ Word the questions effectively.
Try to avoid phrases that might lead the other person to believe you are implying something, or you are questioning their knowledge. Avoid questions that might convey negative feelings.

♦ Ensure proper timing.
To ask the right questions at the wrong time can turn out to be costly.

- Know the other party's personality style and select your line of questioning accordingly.

- Funnel you questions from the broad and general level to the more specific details.

- Build on previous information.
  Listen to all the answers very carefully, and use important material to help build your next question.

- Repeat the question.

Example

"We don't use XYZ company as our manufacturer anymore."
"You don't use XYZ anymore?"
"No, we found that ABC company can provide us with the same quality at a twelve-percent lower price."

This knowledge would, of course lead you to request a lower price for their product at a later point in your negotiations. If the answers are not as explicit as you hoped, ask the other person to restate their answer.

- Ask people who have had prior business dealings with this particular company. You would not believe how extensive some descriptions can be. It is usually much easier to get information at a face to face meeting than over the phone.

It is very important not to let the person you ask get the feeling that you are there solely to question them. Try to establish rapport and make people feel comfortable talking to you. The quality and quantity of valuable information will depend on it.

Keep your questioning non-threatening at all times. You have to keep the communication channels open. Intimidating questions and inquiries that are too personal, are counter-productive, since the other party will put up his guard and clam up.

Sometimes, however, you will have to ask very personal questions. A real estate agent, for example, has to find out how high the income and how great the debt of a potential buyer are. In that case, prepare the other party: For his own benefit, and in order to proceed successfully, you will have to ask a few personal questions. This way the other party will feel he is being interviewed rather than interrogated. As long as you are gentle with your questioning, the communication channels will remain open.

B. Listening

The most important factor in the quest for information is to listen. The more you get the other party to talk about their needs, the smoother the negotiation phase will be. People generally like to talk. By encouraging them to lay down all their concerns and expectations in front of you, they become more comfortable doing business with you.

At the same time, you are gathering valuable information. This will help you prepare a successful strategy and you will stay in control. Never forget, however, that you are also only human. You share the same desire to talk. Realize this at all times and force yourself from time to time to stop talking and start listening.

Effective listening skills have to be acquired. Your ears might hear what somebody is saying, but your brain has to analyze the actual meaning. A careful evaluation of a message can provide you with valuable clues about the other party.

A common mistake during negotiations is that people tend to use their listening time to prepare what they will say next. By doing so, information that could prove to be helpful later in the negotiation process will be missed. Tape-record yourself and you will realize how difficult it is to listen. It requires an abundance of self discipline and proper motivation.

Do not interrupt the other person. We all know that this is very impolite and definitely not appreciated, nevertheless we still do it from time to time. Remember that by interrupting you might miss a vital piece of information the other party wants to tell you.

Support your listening by taking notes. Even if you feel you have a good memory it is still a good idea to do this. Remember that the dullest pencil is better than the sharpest memory. Develop an efficient technique on taking notes, while retaining what is being said.

Look for signals other than the spoken word. How is the other person's eye contact? If he or she rarely makes eye contact, you should have doubts about his or her truthfulness. Look for other non-verbal messages that are (subconsciously) sent your way. Your counterparts might say one thing while their body language is telling you something different.

It is influential to send positive body signals yourself, such as maintaining eye contact, etc. To become a successful negotiator it is important to understand body language. I will address this topic in more detail in chapter XI.

Maintain a pleasant and friendly environment throughout your negotiations. This will require you to respond strictly to the messages and to avoid making personal issues out of them. Instead of getting angry at the person who made an (in your opinion) unacceptable statement, find out why he or she feels that way. By doing so, you might locate compromises acceptable to both of you.

Always control your emotions! If you get upset, you give away your controlling position. I already mentioned the advantage of maintaining the controlling lead role in negotiations. Getting angry hinders your ability to think logically, and it will strongly impair your problem-solving process.

As a negotiator you will have to work on suppressing anger and animosity towards your opponent. Other emotions have similar effects. We all know the saying, "Love is blind." Reports that a sudden outbreak of love interfered with a negotiation, however, are rather scarce.

C. Choice of Location

The location you choose for information gathering is also quite significant. People are usually more willing to share information in a neutral and more relaxed environment. Meeting in a street cafe and conducting the initial round of negotiations over a cappuccino has worked for me numerous times.

Aim to establish an atmosphere with little or no distraction. Distractions will cause poor listening which, in turn, might result in communication problems.

5. Introduce Solutions

This is the core of any negotiation. After you have completed all your preliminary work, it is time to identify mutually acceptable solutions. Decide whether sufficient common denominators exist to make compromises possible. It is sometimes better just to walk away from a hopeless situation.

Most likely, however, you will find a wide enough base for both parties to build their negotiations on. This is the point where actual negotiation techniques will come into play.

People who search actively for creative alternatives will be more successful than those who don't focus on a wide enough spectrum of possible solutions. How to reach a compromise will be covered in detail in the remaining chapters.

V

SMOOTH SELLING

Despite the fact that people usually dislike sales people, selling remains a determining factor in every business operation, as well in everybody's private lives. There is no industry that does not sell a product or service. Every time you are interviewed for a new position, or you ask for a raise, you are selling yourself. Whether you get the job or the raise depends on how well you market yourself.

When I first became involved in real estate, I could not come to terms with the thought of selling. So I developed my own, more consultative approach. I sorted out all the typical sales gambits that I learned, and kept only those techniques that felt comfortable.

A very useful method to detect and disarm objections and concerns is the CEIC approach:

1. Clarify

Verify whether you truly understand the other party's concern. This serves, not to question your intelligence, but to help

---

eliminate possible misunderstandings and misinterpretations from the beginning. You can clarify in many ways. Here are some examples:

"If I understand you correctly, you ...."
"Are you saying that ....?"
"Could you elaborate on this concern?"

That will help you identify the problem. Several sales trainers recommend to clarify by simply restating the concern:

Example

Customer: "I don't think I am interested in two-story homes"

Salesperson: "So, you are saying that you are not interested in a two-story house?"

I find this crude way of clarifying very unappealing and even disturbing. It makes the salesperson appear ignorant, to say the least. My recommendation is to not plainly repeat, but to show more creativity in paraphrasing the original statement.

2. Empathize

Show your counterpart that you respect his or her opinion, and that you can relate to all concerns.

Examples

"I can understand why you feel that way."
"I can appreciate that. Many people have the same concern."
"That is a reasonable objection."

This form of dignifying concerns helps to establish good rapport. People like empathetic remarks that acknowledge their feelings.

3. Isolate

Find out if this is the only concern blocking an agreement. If you accommodate a customer by complying with his or her objection, without prior isolation of the problem, you might find yourself confronted with another objection that you will have to deal with.

Example

"Besides the cost, would you be interested in this product?" or "If we could deliver it in less than twenty days, would you be interested?"

4. Confirm

If all objections have been addressed and a compromise has been presented, it is important to confirm the buyer's commitment.

Example

"If we commit ourselves to deliver within fifteen days, will this be satisfactory to you?" or "If we would additionally provide a complimentary one-year maintenance commitment, would that help finalize our negotiations?"

There are many other sales approaches in common use, many of which I find very unappealing. As I already mentioned, I developed a sales philosophy much different to the commonly known sales tactics. I am not saying that all traditional sales techniques are wrong and should not be used, I just prefer the consultative and less "pushy" approach. Portraying the image of the supportive consultant suits my personality style better than the conception of the hard-core sales person.

Sometimes, during sales presentations, when I sense a lack of interest or resentment from the client, I practice a "negative" sales approach:

I close my file and say to my prospect: "You seem to be not really interested in this product/service. I am sorry if I am boring you." This tactic always confuses a potential customer, because it is a totally unexpected action. The client will most likely re-open the negotiation, and my chances of closing the deal will swiftly increase.

VI

WHAT MAKES A SUCCESSFUL NEGOTIATOR?

1. Be Prepared

Any negotiation session is a unique encounter that requires thought and planning. How well you do at the bargaining table depends on how prepared you are. The negotiation process does not begin when you and your counterpart sit down to inform each other what you want to accomplish. It starts when you do your research.

Know exactly what you want and plan ahead for all eventualities. You have to know which concessions and compromises you are willing to accept. To be an effective negotiator, you have to have a game plan. I recommend a plan consisting of three levels:

1. The absolute minimum you must be able to gain.
2. What you would like to get out of the negotiations?
3. What would be a great bonus to get?

Once you have established your plan, run through every possible "what-if" scenario. This way you will be prepared for everything your opponent might throw at you. To avoid hasty decisions (sometimes even panic) it is advisable to have a backup plan readily available.

Knowing your bottom line helps you to avoid accepting an offer that you might regret later.

2. Understand Negotiating Pressure

Always keep in mind that negotiating pressures both parties equally.

Example

It is only human to be very intimidated when applying for a bank loan. You sit across from a grim faced man with horn-rimmed glasses, hoping to meet all necessary requirements. You perceive the situation as LITTLE YOU against the BIG BANKER. What you don't know is that in his staff meeting that morning, the bank's vice president warned all loan agents that if their lending amounts didn't increase, they would face layoffs. So, this grim-faced man across from you may want to grant you a loan just as much as you want to get it. Never assume that the negotiation pressure is only on you!

3. Learn Negotiation Tactics

It is essential to have the desire to learn negotiation techniques. You have already shown your desire to learn about negotiation techniques by reading this book. Congratulations!

4. Practice Negotiation Tactics

After studying this book, practice your negotiation tactics. Start with trivial everyday situations.

You can practice these techniques when you:

- Negotiate the room rate in a hotel.
- Buy or sell something through a classified ad in the newspaper.
- Experience bad service in a restaurant, etc.

5. Build Trust

The more someone trusts you, the smoother the negotiations will proceed. Conversely, if your opponent does not trust you, it will be very difficult to reach a compromise.

The other party will second-guess everything you say. It will be exceptionally hard to achieve concessions.

Here are a few suggestions on building trust:

Say what you will do, and do what you promised!

This rule contains two valuable parts. First, you should inform your counterpart what your next steps will be. In chapter VIII of this book, I explain the effects that withholding information can have. In this instance, it would most likely be a negative effect and should not be exercised. People feel uncomfortable when they are left in the dark. If you are trying to build trust, make your opponent feel as content as possible. Be careful, however, that you don't get carried away and promise more than you will actually be able to do.

That brings us to the second part of this rule: Keep your promises. If you agreed to discount your price by ten percent, you will have to stick with it. If you are not sure that such a discount would be feasible for you, leave it open. Say something like "I would like to give you a discount, but let me first make a few calculations before I commit myself to an exact figure."

Don't be a stickler

We all know that everybody makes mistakes. Remember this when your counterpart trips over a mistake that he or she made. If it was an honest mistake, allow your opponent to make proper corrections when revising the proposal. This will be seen as a very accommodating gesture, and will help you build trust.

Admit when you are wrong

No matter how skilled you are, you are bound to make a mistake at some point. Instead of attempting to cover it up, be open about it. Admitting your mistake will strengthen your credibility.

Don't ask for trust!

Building trust cannot be accomplished if you flat out ask the other party to trust you. Phrases such as, "You know you can trust me." or "Let me assure you, I am being perfectly honest with you." are commonly used by people who mean exactly the opposite of what they are saying.

You cannot ask for trust, you have to earn it by being open and straightforward. Questionable approaches, such as these phrases, will hinder the trust-building process. Chapter IX will explain commonly used phrases and their true meaning in more detail.

6. Don't Just Talk, Communicate!

Clear communication is a vital prerequisite to successful negotiating. Many negotiations fell apart simply because the parties were unable to establish and maintain open communications. Communicating is generally much more complex and difficult than people realize. The typical problem during negotiations is emotional involvement. When people get caught up in their own web of emotions, and only think about what they want, they often fail to express themselves clearly. They stop listening to what the other party has to say and they talk past each other. Instead of a prosperous dialogue, the parties engage in parallel monologues, which will inevitably lead to misinterpretations and misunderstandings.

The key factors are to say what you really mean, in a way that it presents your case as strongly as possible, and to take time to actively listen to what your counterpart has to say. Remember that it is perfectly alright to take a minute to collect your thoughts and to think through the offer just made to you. Asking for a longer time-out is better than rushing to a wrong conclusion. Buying time will help you to not only better prepare your response, it will also give you time to digest the true meaning of what the other party proposed.

To become successful in your negotiations you have to think ahead as many moves as possible. Just like a seasoned chess player, it is necessary to think of what response your counterpart may have to your proposal. Predicting your opponent's responses will be more difficult in some situations than others, but it always pays off to think ahead.

The next criteria of concise communication is to keep the other party interested in what you have to say. Since every negotiation process entails desirable aspects for both parties, it is advantageous to emphasize the benefits for the other party, even while you are stating what you want. Always stress the value and not the cost to your counterpart.

Example

When you are on a job interview, focus on all the benefits you would be able to provide to the company. Convince them that because of your special skills and your extensive experience you would be able to help them outperform their competition. Once the other party realizes the advantages you could bring, they will be more willing to make concessions, such as salary and other benefits.

7. Create Win-Win Solutions

Almost every type of business generates most of it's revenue through repeat business. Don't sacrifice a business relationship that has potential to yield a high amount of future business for an advantage in your present negotiations. Remember the importance of win-win negotiations as explained in Chapter III.

VII

NEGOTIATION TACTICS

1.   Higher Authority

Many people have an uncontrollable urge to announce that they have unlimited authority to negotiate. Their egos crave this acknowledgment of power. From the moment the other party knows that you are ultimately in charge of any decision making, you have given away one of the most effective negotiation tactics: the Higher Authority method.

In my consulting business, I am frequently contacted by all kinds of sales people. During my first year as an entrepreneur, I was so proud to be the decision-maker in my company, that the thought of disguising this fact never even crossed my mind; I became easy prey for seasoned sales persons. Eventually I realized my mistake. From that point on, I was in greater control of all negotiations with sales representatives.

Example

"Let me present this to my partners in next week's meeting. Why don't you call me Thursday of next week and I will tell you what my partners think about your proposal." When the sales representative calls me, I can tell him: "I tried to sell your plan to my business partners, but they feel that your price is higher than they are willing to pay. However, they authorized me to sign the agreement if you can lower the price by 15 percent." Chances are, the sales person will be more inclined to take the offer at 15 percent less, than to wait for further proposals and counterproposals to get through my board of directors.

The most efficient way to implement the Higher Authority method is by the use of a very vague entity. Committees, boards of directors, or commissions are ideal. This technique is favored because one can put pressure on the other party without assuming the role of the confrontational "bad guy." Since many people know about this tactic, you can easily find yourself in a position where somebody uses the Higher Authority method on you. To prevent that from happening, it is essential to confirm your counterpart's eligibility to make a decision without anybody else's approval right from the start. Phrases like: "If we can reach an agreement, will you be able to make a decision today?"

In some cases, the answer might be: "No, I will have to present it to our committee and I will need their approval." To counter that, I try to address the other person's ego by saying: "I understand, but I am sure they will follow your recommendation. You will recommend it?"

If somebody asks you, if you will be able to make a decision today, you can disarm your counterpart by responding: "That depends on the price. If you can lower the price to $3,000, I would have the necessary authority to make a decision without my board's approval."

Another option of dealing with a Higher Authority would be the Contingency or Rescission methods: "I understand that you have to get your committee's approval on this. We both know that you will get their okay anyway. Why don't we set up the contract right now and make it contingent on your committee's approval within the next three days." Or better yet: "Let's set up the contract right now and give your committee the option to cancel the contract within three days."

If there is a legitimate Higher Authority involved in the decision making process, you have to follow these three steps:

1. Identify the Higher Authority by verifying its form and actual decision-making power. Find out whether it is a board of directors, a finance committee, business partners, etc. Further, determine how much impact it will have in the negotiation process.

2. Talk directly to the decision-making entity. Invite yourself to the next board meeting, for example. Don't let others negotiate for you. If you have to rely on someone else to communicate on your behalf, you put yourself in a powerless position.

3. When you are making a presentation to committees, take time to talk to each person involved in the decision making. Listen to his or her concerns in this matter. Once you know each individual's concerns, you can address these issues, and you will be able to demonstrate how you can ensure that each concern will be met.

2. Good Guy-Bad Guy

Everybody knows about the Good Guy-Bad Guy tactic. We have seen this gambit used many times in movies and on TV where one detective interrogates a suspect and treats him rather harshly. When he leaves the room, another detective, who was completely passive throughout the entire line of questioning by his colleague, approaches the suspect. He acts very cordial and helpful.

He offers the guy a cigarette and says: "I am sorry, I know my partner is a loose cannon. Why don't you let me help you? Just tell me what you know and I will make sure my partner stays away from you." That is the classic "Good Cop - Bad Cop" method.

Despite the fact that this particular technique is so well known, it still works and is used effectively every day. You probably have already noticed a certain similarity between this technique and the Higher Authority method.

If you find yourself in a situation where two sales people are trying this technique on you, watch out for the "good guy." You must always remember that the "good guy" is definitely not on your side!

Example

I was making a presentation to a board of directors. At one point during the negotiations one director stood up and expressed angrily that he felt the negotiations were going nowhere because we were way too far apart on price. He stormed out of the room. You could sense the tension in the room. Another director looked at me and said in an amicable tone: "I feel we have come a long way in our negotiations. I am sure we can bring the price to a level that our entire board can feel comfortable with."

Example

Car salesmen like to use the Good Guy-Bad Guy technique. At first, they seem to agree with your offer, but tell you that the final okay has to come from the manager. When they return from the manager's office, they often say something like: "He didn't approve it, but he said, that we are really close."

To counter this tactic, you can fight fire with fire and use the very same technique on your opponent. In this case, for example, your spouse could assume the role of the "Bad Guy" by disapproving of spending one dollar more than the price previously discussed.

Another very effective way to counter the Good Guy-Bad Guy routine, is through plain embarrassment. Questions such as: "Are you really trying to play Good Guy-Bad Guy with me?" should accomplish just that.

3. Nibbling

This tactic is based upon the theory that you can still negotiate one or two more concessions, even after an agreement has been reached.

After the initial agreement has been reached, a certain psychological effect kicks in: Everyone feels comfortable because they have accomplished something. This is the precise moment when the Nibbling technique can be used effectively.

Example

Picture yourself in a situation where you are laying the groundwork with a new employer. You have agreed on salary, benefits, expense account, authority, and other factors. You shake hands and start to leave the room. Before reaching the door, you turn for one more statement — TV inspector Columbo's trademark.

"And I am certain you understand that as the new vice president of marketing I of course will need a membership in the country club to entertain current and potential clients?" Chances are the answer will be "yes." If you would have made your request part of the original negotiations, you might have ended up with fewer benefits, lower salary, or a reduced expense account to compensate for your country club membership.

The important part of Nibbling is to "feel" when to nibble and how much to nibble. If you ask for too much, you will not get it and you will leave a negative impression. Remember, this technique is called Nibbling, not Gulping!

Example

When I shopped for a new computer for my home office, I decided on a model priced at $2,199. I asked the sales person if he could upgrade the memory from eight to sixteen megabytes at no extra charge. After the sales clerk agreed, I said I would be by the following day to finalize everything.

The next day, I told the sales person that I would be willing to purchase the computer system, if he would include additional software. After agreeing, I told him I would have my office issue a check, and I would pick up the computer that afternoon.

When I went back that afternoon, I told the sales clerk: "My boss is such a cheapskate! He issued a check for $2,100 and said that would be the most he is willing to spend."

I purchased the computer with upgraded memory and with additional software, for only $2,100.

The interesting, yet complex facet of negotiation gambits is, that for almost every tactic, a counter-move exists. There is also a counter-move to Nibbling: The best thing to do, is to make the other person feel cheap.

In our example, the counter-move might result in an answer such as: "Oh, come on! You negotiated the best terms I have ever agreed to. Don't make me give you another $30,000 for a country club membership!"

Another effective method to stop Nibbling is to nibble back! Soon, your counterparts will realize that it would be best to close the negotiations before they begin losing what they have negotiated.

4. Hot Potato

This situation occurs when somebody passes a potential problem on to you.

Example

When I was in real estate, I was approached by a customer interested in buying a four bedroom home, not older than five years, with a large backyard in one of Denver's nicest areas. The hot potato that he tossed me was that he could only spend up to $150,000. Locating such a property for less than $200,000 was totally unrealistic.

The first thing you should do when somebody tosses you a hot potato is to find out how "hot" the potato actually is. Many times the problem will prove to be a lot less genuine than initially presented.

Back to our example: I told the customer that I knew of two properties that would meet his requirements, but they were both in the $200,000 range. I asked if he would be at all interested to see them, or if we should not bother looking at them.

"Well," he said, "I might be able to afford that price range, if the home is exactly what my wife and I are looking for."

So the hot potato turned out to be not hot at all. Imagine how much time and money I could have wasted, by trying to find such a property under $150,000! I would probably have searched for weeks without finding anything. But having examined the situation, I was able to start right away showing the buyer an array of homes in the $200,000 range. Within the first week we wrote an offer on a property listed for $214,000.

5.   Detour

You will find this technique somewhat similar to the Hot Potato technique. If one party states: "Our company would be interested in doing business with you, but only if you could cut your price to $50 per piece." the Detour Method might be appropriate.

Even if you cannot lower your price per unit to $50 without accepting a loss, don't get tangled up in explaining your position and discussing the price issue. The proper approach would be to say: "Let's not talk about price right now. Why don't we first find out where we stand on all the other issues?"

Once your opponent agrees to other issues, you have created a certain drive for further agreements to follow. This is one of the foundations in negotiating: Little decisions lead to big decisions. Very often you will find that the opening statement of not being willing to pay over $50 per unit is not necessarily written in stone. You might walk away with $65 per unit, a price that is much more acceptable to you.

6.   The Limbo

An important key question in any negotiation about price is to find out how low your counterpart is willing to go. *How low can you go?* That's why I call this gambit "The Limbo."

It takes some practice to learn how to read people. However, it is an essential element of the negotiation process to know what price the other person has in mind as the absolute minimum.

Example

You would like to buy a sailboat, someone advertised in the paper. It is listed for $6,000. When you meet with the seller you ask: "What would be the lowest price you would sell it for?" He responds: "Well, for you I would sell it for $5,500." Without any haggling he has already dropped the price by $500. This is a good sign. If someone lowers his asking price substantially, without any negotiating effort, you know you can easily get the price down even farther.

Observe how long it takes your opponent to offer you a lower price, how much or little negotiation effort on your part was necessary to achieve this. Most of all, keep an eye on the amount of the price reduction. If you learn how to read these indications, you have gained an important advantage from the beginning.

7.   The Trial Balloon

Every decent negotiator enters a negotiation only after setting the absolute minimum or maximum figure for the transaction. Let's refer to this number as the "secret number." It would be so much easier to achieve success in your negotiations, if you knew what your opponent's secret number was.

One way to find out roughly what the other party's secret number might be is to send a "Trial Balloon."

Example

One of my real estate clients was interested in a property that was listed at $224,900. We decided to send up a trial balloon: I called the listing agent and told him that I had a buyer who was interested in the property. I told him that he was pre-qualified up to $210,000 and that was as high as he could go. "Would it still be worth our time to look at this house under these circumstances?" I asked.

Sending up a trial balloon usually results in one of three responses:

1. "No, I don't believe the seller would be willing to reduce the price that much"

   Response: "Well, exactly how willing would he be?" Do you recognize this approach? It's the limbo.

2. "No, the seller would definitely not lower the price below $220,000."

   This tells you that the secret number lies probably between $215,000 and $220,000. With this knowledge you have already gained the leading edge in these negotiations.

3. "Yes, when would you like to show the property?"

   This response is very rare. If a trial balloon is being accepted right away, you should examine the situation very carefully to see that there are no hidden pitfalls waiting for you. Remember one of the ground rules of negotiating: Never accept a first offer. (See Chapter II)

There are also Trial Balloon phrases that can help you learn more about the other party. Here are a few examples that can start a sentence:

What would happen, if we ...
I haven't given it a lot of thought, but ...
Off the top of my head, I would say that ...

The person sending one of these trial balloons already has a plan, or at least a suggestion of one, but he or she is unsure what the other party's response will be. Such a trial balloon can tell an experienced negotiator that the party who made the suggestion, hidden in their trial balloon, would be willing to accept the solution they are recommending. It is furthermore an indication that due to their doubts of your acceptance, you will be able to negotiate an even better deal.

8. Feel-Felt-Found

The best way to take the wind out of someone's sails is to agree with them. This surprise factor will force them to alter their approach and will give you instant opportunity to take control of the discussion.

Example

Real estate agents install combination lockboxes on the homes they have for sale. These lockboxes can be opened by real estate agents who want to show the property to a potential buyer. During a listing appointment, my sellers said they would not allow a lockbox on their home. They feared for their valuable gun collection and for their paintings, and they were afraid that a lockbox would allow too many people to have access to their home.

"I can certainly understand your concern," I replied. "If I had such valuables in my house, I would FEEL exactly the same way. Many other sellers also FELT very uncomfortable about giving strangers access to their house. But we have FOUND, that without a lockbox you will lose approximately 70 percent of all potential buyers."

After a few more explanations, the sellers agreed to a lockbox installation on their house, and placed their gun collection and their paintings in storage.

9. Walk Away Power

The worst thing that can happen to you during a negotiation is that your opponent realizes that you are determined to close the deal at all cost. Once your opponent knows that you can't or won't walk away from this deal, you will end up paying a higher price. It is essential to never rule out the option to walk away from a negotiation if you don't feel comfortable with the terms. Demonstrated walk-away power will give you significant leverage throughout your negotiations.

An apparent walk-away attitude can also become part of your negotiation gambit:

Example

A few years ago, I helped a friend of mine with his purchase of a new home. He was interested in a particular property that was listed for $230,000. After we negotiated for several days, the seller reduced his asking price to $226,000, which was still $3,000 more than my client wanted to pay.

My friend and I decided to give it one more try, but even if we were not successful, he would be willing to settle for the latest asking price of $226,000. I called the listing agent and told her that, since the buyer and the seller do not seem to be able to agree on a price, we would have to withdraw our offer. Our apparent willingness to walk away from these negotiations resulted in an additional price reduction by the seller. My buyer ended up purchasing the home for only $224,000.

10. The Gatekeeper

When negotiations stretch for an extended period of time, some negotiators try to use this tactic to buy time and gain control.

It is only possible to make progress in negotiations, when you can talk directly to a decision maker. Secretaries who screen incoming calls and keep certain people from talking to their bosses are typical of gatekeepers.

Sales people get very frustrated when they get stopped by a gatekeeper and cannot get through to the decision maker.

Meanwhile, their counterpart has time to prepare himself for the next round of negotiations. Use of a gatekeeper takes control away from the sales person. It is his opponent who decides if and when to make himself available for further discussions.

Some secretaries add even more zest to this technique by including the "Good Guy-Bad Guy" tactic to their role as a gatekeeper. By acting as the "Good Guy," they can obtain vital information from the sales person. They will side with the frustrated sales person and promise to put a good word in for them with their boss.

Counters for this tactic are, unfortunately, very limited. First try to bypass the gatekeeper by calling during the gate keeper's lunch break, or by insisting to hold the line instead of waiting for the boss to call you back. If this proves to be unsuccessful, consider exercising your walk-away power and end the negotiations.

11. Competition

Unless you are negotiating with a company that holds an absolute monopoly position on a specific product, you will always be able to find a competitor who sells a comparable if not identical product. Use this element in your negotiations.

Example

"I realize this is a great product, that's why I am interested in a possible purchase. My only concern is your price. I found two of your competitors selling the same product up to fifteen percent less than you. Would you be able to match their offer?"

Quite often, your opponent will be willing to match the competitor's price right away. The fear of losing business to a competitor is not only a financial matter, it's a matter of pride.

You can also create such a situation by bluffing. There might not even be a competitor who is discounting this product up to fifteen percent. Unless your counterpart really knows the market so well that he will call your bluff, you may get away with it. But isn't that considered "lying?" No! It is considered "successful negotiating."

Example

You are shopping for a new car. A salesman tells you his "best" price is $21,000.

You tell the salesman: "Another dealership has already offered to sell me the same car for $19,750 and I did not buy it then." You turn around and walk away. The salesperson comes after you with the offer of $19,250 if you buy today. All you did was combine the two negotiation principles of Competition and Walk Away Power. They helped you get the price reduced by $1,750. Not bad for about three minutes worth of work.

12. Flinching

This technique is so basic that it amazes me every time I see it implemented effectively.

Example

A sales representative from a local TV station was making a presentation. She suggested a certain air-time package for $4,000. At that moment I felt it was a good time to "flinch."

"Four thousand dollars?" I complained. She immediately tried to straighten out this situation and responded: "But we would be willing to give you the commercial production at no cost. We would usually charge $500 for such a production." She would never have made this offer without my flinch.

If you think that the asking price of $4,000 is quite reasonable, make sure to never express it. If the other party realizes that you feel comfortable with the asking price, you will be surprised how quickly little extra costs will be added on.

Some people feel that it is below their dignity to flinch. When they ask how much the price of a particular new car is and the salesman answers, "Nineteen thousand dollars." they might say: "That seems very reasonable." At that point the salesman will charge them for all the extras they might want.

If they would have responded with a flinch and said: "That much? It's a little more than we expected." the salesman's response would have been quite different: "Yes, but this includes many extras!" They could have instantly saved hundreds, maybe thousands of dollars.

Once you practice this technique, you will find out that it pays to flinch!

If you are in a position where you have to fight off someone's flinch, defend your product or service for what it is worth. Many people flinch, not because they are experienced negotiators, but because they lack knowledge about your product's quality, the production cost, etc. Before you give up too much due to your counterpart's flinch, first try to justify your price. You can always offer a discount later on.

13. The Shotgun

Once in a while you will encounter this tactic when one party is trying to force his opponent into agreeing with his demands. This technique very often includes a non-negotiable demand. It is also commonly referred to as a "take it or leave it" approach.

I would recommend reserving this technique for very rare and special situations. In many cases, the shotgun tactic will not lead to a win-win outcome. The person using the shotgun method will either be winner or all negotiations will end immediately. The two possible outcomes would be a win-lose or a lose-lose situation.

The shotgun tactic is primarily used by someone who thinks that he or she will eventually find a buyer who is willing to meet all demands. A person with no time limit for a particular sale will do well with this technique. But then again, who has absolutely no time limit?

14.   The Trade-off

There are times in the negotiating process that it becomes clear to you that you must make a concession for the negotiations to succeed at all. At this point it would be advantageous to give in and to make the concession. Right after this compromise, however, it is time for a trade-off. You want the other party to give up something that would benefit you in return.

The trade-off principle has a high success rate in negotiations, provided that the timing is right. The odds for a successful trade-off result will decrease rapidly from the moment you made your initial concession. It is essential to ask for your requested trade-off immediately, because the value of a concession or of a service tends to diminish rather rapidly in the eyes of a buyer as time passes.

Example

Once, I was checking in at a Marriott hotel where I had reservations for a room with a king-size bed. The front desk agent was very apologetic when she told me that all king-size rooms were taken, and she could only accommodate me in a room with two queen-size beds.

Since I was travelling alone, it really did not matter whether I stay in a room with king- or queen-size beds. However, I sensed the opportunity to negotiate a trade-off concession.

"This is rather disappointing," I said, "Even my confirmation slip indicates a king-size room. If I would agree to settle for a queen-size room, what could you do for this inconvenience?"

"We would be happy to discount your room rate by 20 percent," she replied. "... And we would also like to bring a complimentary bottle of wine to your room."

Not a bad trade-off! And all I had to do was ask for it.

People who fail to ask for such a trade-off immediately after they agreed to a demand of their counterpart will find themselves quickly losing ground.

15. The "Do Better" Technique

When somebody makes an offer to you, you can apply some pressure simply by responding: "I'm sure you can do better than that!" As unsubstantial as this response actually is, it puts tension on the other person.

If somebody applies this technique to you, answer with this counter: "Exactly how much better do you want me to do?" That pins your opponent down to an exact dollar figure or to certain terms in your negotiations. This method is also known as "The Vise."

Example

A friend of mine teaches at a junior high school. She told me that she used the "Do Better" technique not too long ago when she did not find time to grade the class' reports. She handed the unreviewed reports back to the students, saying that she was very disappointed with the results, and that she was positive that everybody could do better.

When she received the new and improved versions of the report a few days later, she could not believe the high quality of her students' papers. Everybody had done significantly better than usual.

16. The Written Advantage

People tend to believe everything they read in the newspaper. This is not because newspapers are proven to be an ultimately reliable source of authentic information. It is due to the fact that written material is usually very powerful. The written word will be questioned much less often than the spoken word. You can use this truth in your negotiations.

Example

A good way to convey to a longtime customer that the price of your product has gone up is to put it in writing. Hand him a letter with all the necessary information regarding the price increase and say: "I received this notification from our headquarters last week." This way, you not only use the power of the written word, but also the technique of higher authority that was discussed previously.

Another advantage of the written word is to become the party in charge of preparing the final contract. Once the negotiations have come to a consensus, a contract is usually drawn up. It can be very advantageous to be nominated to draw up such a document. Some details will always remain that were not finalized during the negotiations.

This allows the person writing the contract to interpret certain technicalities more favorably. It would now be up to the other party to address those points and to ask for changes. Very often, they will simply agree with the contract and sign it in its original form.

Here is a third advantage of having things in writing: Let's say you are very close in your negotiations, but nothing has been confirmed yet. You take it upon yourself to set up a contract reflecting all the negotiated arrangements. All those little details that allow room for interpretation have been interpreted in your favor. You enclose your payment and deliver it to the other party.

Now they have to decide which option to choose:

A. They can reject the contract because of certain details they might not agree with. That means that they have to refund your payment and risk the whole deal falling apart.

B. They can accept the contract as-is, cash your check, and focus on their next business project.

I think you see that many times option B will be preferred. This tactic is often referred to as "fait accompli," which means, "It is done."

17. The Withdrawn Offer

This technique works very well in situations where your opponent is grinding your price down lower and lower.

Example

A sales representative of a tool manufacturing company is negotiating the price per unit of a certain tool. The buyer turns out to be a very tough negotiator and has already accomplished a reduction from $1.75 to $1.45 per unit. Since the salesman's negotiation range ends at $1.40 per tool, he has to think of a way to stop the ongoing discounting process. The buyer's last offer was $1.45, but even if the salesman agrees to this price, the buyer may try to get a better deal.

The sales representative's response is: "I think we can arrange to give you the tool at $1.45 per unit, but let me present it to our vice president of sales to get it approved. I will get back to you tomorrow."

The next day, when he meets with the buyer, he says: "Our vice president recalculated all the figures and he found that at a price of $1.45 per unit we would cut way too deep into our profit margin. He said that $1.50 per unit is the best we can do." (Did you notice he used the Higher Authority method?)

The buyer counters, somewhat upset: "Yesterday you felt that we could settle for $1.45 and today it is $1.50! If you can guarantee $1.45 per unit, I am willing to place my order today."

The salesman makes a phone call (supposedly to his boss). When he returns he tells the buyer that he tried his best to convince the vice president to agree to the price of $1.45.

He did, but only under the condition that the buyer increase his order from 10,000 to 12,000 pieces. "Would that be acceptable?"

Looking back at this transaction, we can see that the sales representative not only stayed well within his negotiation range, but also managed to increase his sales volume by twenty percent. Remember that all this started simply with a Withdrawn Offer.

18.   Funny Money

This principle involves the technique of converting the actual price into unrealistic small increments.

Example

An encyclopedia salesman tried to sell me a comprehensive set of encyclopedias for less than 36 cents a day. Since this amount sounds very reasonable for virtually everybody's pocketbook, many people might be tempted to agree to the purchase without actually thinking of the actual price. Less than 36 cents a day over the average life span of the encyclopedia set of 15 years would amount to $2,000.

Car sales people are specialists in Funny Money. Rather than telling you the total price of the car, they tell you that it is only $349 per month.

To counter such Funny Money negotiations, simply insist on total figures or you will walk away.

19. The Decoy and The Dead Fish

This tactic is used to distract the opponent from the real issue by throwing in a so-called Decoy. You basically make a big deal out of an issue that in reality does not mean very much to you.

Example

After all details have been worked out between you and the other party, you learn that it will take four to six weeks to deliver the merchandise. Although waiting does not really matter to you, it is a great opportunity to throw a Decoy.

"I was expecting to have the merchandise delivered within two to three weeks. This unexpected long delivery time would inconvenience our operations substantially. We are willing to go through with a delivery time that long, if you could give us a five percent discount." Chances are, you will be able to negotiate additional advantages as a tradeoff for something that really was not important to you anyway.

The Dead Fish is a special form of a Decoy. Where the Decoy more or less offers itself during a negotiation, the Dead Fish is intentionally planted into a negotiation process, only to be withdrawn again at a later point. By bringing a Dead Fish into your negotiations, you are asking for something that you know will be unacceptable to your opponent. After you have caused enough confusion and upset, you withdraw your Dead Fish, but of course, not without trading it off for a valuable concession from your opponent.

This technique is also referred to as the *Red Herring Tactic*. The name for this negotiation gambit originated from old English fox hunting competitions. One team would drag a dead fish across the fox's path in order to make the dogs of the opposing team lose the trail.

If you recognize that someone is applying this maneuver on you, try to disarm it by using the Detour method, as explained earlier in this chapter.

20.   The Puppy Dog Close

This technique derives from a pet store owner who is trying to sell a fairly expensive dog to a customer and his son. The little boy showed an instant liking to the dog, but the father was somewhat apprehensive to pay so much money. That's when the pet store owner suggested that they should take the dog home and keep it over the weekend. If they decide that they don't want it, they can bring the dog back on Monday, and their money would be refunded. Of course, the parents would not return the dog because their son grew attached to the puppy over the weekend.

You can also find this technique among car dealers. They sometimes let the customer test drive the new car over the weekend, hoping they will get so attached to the vehicle that they will purchase it by the time Monday comes.

21. The "Ask For More" Tactic

Experienced negotiators know how important it is to start out asking for much more than they expect to get. This is to keep your adversary busy wrestling with your unreasonable proposal so that you can confer a feeling of satisfaction to the opposing party by finally reducing your original proposal.

Don't be surprised if, when using this tactic, you suddenly end up with a far better deal than you had expected.

Example

When I sat on the board of a corporation in California I presented a proposal to the board of directors. My proposal included eight elements. While three subjects were very important to me, I was willing to negotiate the other five. If I could have gotten the board's approval on only the three important points, I would have considered the meeting a success. To my surprise, the board rejected only one of my eight requests.

22. The First Offer

One of the basic rules in negotiations is to let the other party make the first offer. This puts you in a better position for further negotiations. Sometimes that's not possible, however. It is therefore important to know how you should present the first offer.

Example

If you are interested in buying a boat that is listed for $12,000, you have several negotiation options when making your offer. You could offer $9,000 and tell the seller to take it or leave it. This tactic might work in a few cases. Most often, however, it will antagonize the other party to the point that all negotiations may stop before they actually started.

It would be a more promising tactic to come in with a ridiculously low offer, but show flexibility. "I know that this is a lot less than your asking price, but based on what I have seen, I am willing to pay $8,000 for it."

The fact you are showing flexibility, will convince the seller to spend some time negotiating with you, despite your low-ball offer. Low-balling generally lowers your counterpart's aspirations.

There are several ways to counter a low-ball offer:

A. Stick to your asking price and try to justify it to your opponent.

B. Walk away without making a counter offer.

C. Apply the "Do Better" technique. Sate that the offer is totally unacceptable and that only a drastic improvement could open the negotiations.

23. Facts and Figures

Including facts and figures in your negotiations can be very advantageous. Properly used data can prove to be a very powerful tool, provided that your facts are correct and documentable. People who have statistics readily available to be thrown into their negotiations convey an image of power through knowledge to their counterparts.

At first, the opponents will be skeptical about the information. They will probably try to disarm your arguments by challenging your facts. If you can provide satisfactory documentation and proof of your data, you will score valuable points in the negotiation game.

If one side has more information than the other, it will be a very lopsided round of negotiations; the party that has done more homework will prevail.

Very often I see negotiators using fictional facts and figures. They use this tactic to bluff their way through. Their bluff will be successful as long nobody questions the data, or provides the correct facts. If they do, the bluff will backfire and it will be difficult to regain control of the negotiations. Being well informed is a kind of power that I will address in more detail in Chapter VIII.

24. The Knockout Presentation

The distinct advantage achieved through ample preparation has already been stressed in the previous chapter: Facts and Figures. Another way to impress your counterpart and gain advantage in a negotiation is to make a knockout presentation before the actual negotiation process begins.

Large flow charts, slides, videos, and any other audio visual supports, will always enhance your presentation. Do not let your counterpart get the feeling you are winging it, that you are just speaking off the cuff. To gain negotiation points, you have to demonstrate how thoroughly prepared you are. A well designed presentation will do just that.

Example

In a study, a speaker was asked to give the exact same presentation to ten different groups sequentially. In five of these presentations he was allowed to support his presentation through visual aids.

After each presentation the group had to rate from one to ten (with ten being the highest), how convincing the speaker was. The five groups who saw the presentation without visual aids rated the speaker between five and seven, where the other five groups rated him between six and nine.

25. Splitting the Difference

The prime directive in this matter is to let the other party split the difference. Never offer to split the difference yourself. Here is how it works:

Example

After lengthy negotiations, your offer stands at $12,000. The seller's price has come down to $14,000. Being a good negotiator you know you should never offer to split the difference. You stress the length of time you spent in these negotiations, and outline the compromises both parties have already agreed to.

"Wouldn't it be a shame if we let everything fall apart knowing we are only $2,000 apart?" you ask.

If you present such a statement convincingly and let it then "hang in the room" for a few moments, your opponent will probably suggest splitting the difference. Now you need to confirm that he is reducing his price to $13,000. Your next move should be to ask for an adjournment of the meeting so that you can run this offer by your boss.

The next day you practice the Higher Authority tactic by saying: "I am so sorry, but my boss is really hard to deal with lately. He does not want to pay more than $12,000. We have to do something to close the deal since we are only $1,000 apart." There is a very good chance, the other party is willing to split the difference again. It is your judgement to estimate how often your opponent will split the difference. Before you push it too far and jeopardize the entire transaction, don't hesitate to give in by splitting the last difference yourself.

Remember the importance of attaining win-win solutions, where both parties feel they accomplished their goals.

26.   Sell Cheap, Get Famous

This tactic implies that by selling cheap, or making additional concessions to you now, the person will receive a bigger payoff in the future.

Example

When I first opened a business consulting firm in California, I searched for a reliable graphic designer. I interviewed several businesses and asked them for quotes. Once I decided which company could provide the best services for my needs, I utilized the "Sell Cheap, Get Famous" technique.

I contacted the owner of the company I wanted to do business with and told him that I am was not only looking for a company able to provide high quality services for me, but also for my clients.

"As a business consultant I am looking for a reliable graphic design studio to subcontract all specific marketing needs for my clients. I am expecting the future potential of orders I will provide to you, to be reflected in the price you are quoting me for my order."

Although I lived up to my promise and brought ample business to the designer in my example, people rarely get the reward they are promised. I would advise caution when you are confronted with the "Sell Cheap, Get Famous" technique.

27.　The Seeds of Discord

This method is often used when negotiating with a group of people, such as a committee or a board of directors. The principle behind this tactic is to divide the counterpart's camp.

When negotiating with an entity consisting of several persons, convincing the other side is sometimes very cumbersome. The opposition's negotiation strength is fueled by the fact that they are acting as a unit. Remember the saying: United we stand, divided we fall.

One way to weaken their position would be to break up this unity by dividing them into different opinion groups.

Once the members of the opposing party have been played against each other, the negotiator has successfully sown the seed of discord.

However, I advise to exercise this tactic only as the last resort, due to a very slim success rate. Very often it will lead to a lose/lose outcome, since a divided entity is not likely to agree on anything, and a stalemate will be inevitable.

Personally, I very rarely use this tactic in my negotiations. As you practice the different techniques from this book, you will find yourself favoring some methods more than others. Some gambits will prove to be generally more effective than others, and some will simply harmonize better with your individual personality style.

28.　Time Pressure

The person who has to negotiate under time pressure has a disadvantage. Skilled negotiators very often manage to create a scenario where the other party is facing serious time pressure. And if, in fact, you are facing a deadline to reach an agreement, make sure your opponent remains unaware of the time pressure you are under. Do whatever it takes to disguise your urgency.

When people are pressed for time during a negotiation process, they tend to subconsciously send messages to their counterparts through their body language. Watch for such signs! Chapter XI will provide you with a more information about body language and it's role in negotiations.

You should realize that almost every deadline can be changed or extended. Try to stay calm and patient when you are negotiating. Experience shows that it is unlikely that you will achieve the best possible outcome if you rush it.

As in so many other situations, the Pareto principle, also known as the "80/20 Rule", applies: Eighty percent of the negotiation agreements transpire in the last twenty percent of the time spent negotiating. That is a strong indication of how critical the influence of time is on the outcome of any negotiation.

As a real estate agent I noticed the effect that time has on the willingness to reach an agreement. Even sellers who told me when they signed a listing contract that they would stay firm on the price, started to compromise once an offer was presented. The excitement of closing the sale and the threat of time running out, work as an amazing catalyst to greater willingness to compromise. For this reason, it is essential in any contract to finalize all details at the beginning. The phrase "we can work out the details later," has more often than not caused one party to lose a lot of money.

Children are usually experts in time-pressure negotiations. They had the entire weekend to inform their parents that they need to purchase certain items for school. They, however, always wait until Monday morning to ask for the money. And, of course, they always get away with it, don't they?

29. The Bomb

This principle involves steering your opponent towards the brink of a highly unfavorable outcome. This tactic allows you to use your weight against your counterpart. Your intimidation and your apparent willingness to assume all consequences, will often motivate your opponent enough, that he will comply with your demand. The stakes are high in this gambit, since both parties will suffer a substantial loss if the negotiations fail.

Example

The suggestions to merge with ABC company have been brought up numerous times during the last few meetings of the board of directors of a California corporation. During the actual voting process, eight directors were for, and seven directors (including the chairman) were against the transaction. The chairman, who was ready to accept a decision he did not agree with, chose to use the bomb technique. "If you (directed to the pro voters) will not revise your vote, and force this corporation into a merger, I will resign as your chairman. This would put John Atkinson, president of ABC company, in the chairman position. And we all know that in this case all directors from our corporation will most likely be replaced. Do you really want that, or will you reconsider your decision right now?"

Since the directors didn't want to risk losing their jobs, the motion for a merger was voted down.

30.   The Punt

You occasionally will find that your negotiation tactics don't get the desired results. One way to stir up the opponent's controlling comfort position is by asking "punt" questions. Just like in football, a good punt at the right time can help you score valuable points.

Here are some of the most common punt questions:

> Why do you ask?
> What do you mean by that?
> Is this your final offer?
> So, what are you really saying?
> Do you understand my position?
> Why do you say that?
> Why would I want to do that?

To increase the effectiveness of the punt, follow your question with silence. This will force your opponent to talk, and sometimes they may talk themselves into a corner. Punts don't guarantee that your counterpart will agree to give you what you want, but they will help you shift the momentum in the negotiations to your advantage.

The key factor is the right timing. Choose a point in the negotiation when your counterparts feel that they have you where they want you and then lay it on them.

Asking the right questions at the right time can put you in control of the negotiations. Imagine a court scene, where the prosecutor asks the defendant all kinds of questions and is undoubtedly in full control of the hearing.

Eventually, you will find yourself in a situation where somebody throws a loaded punt your way. How do you counter that? My suggestion would be, to think of another punt question quickly and throw it back in your opponent's corner.

Example

Your counterpart throws you a hot question, such as: "What are your plans if our committee rejects your offer?"
You definitely don't want to tell what your real backup plan is. You would play right into the other party's hands. You can be evasive and say: "I can't disclose that to you." This might do the trick. Another way of countering such an uneasy question would be a simple counter question like: "Why do you ask?"

Either way, you managed to pass the ball back to your opponent, and you stayed in control.

31. Noah's Ark

A closing technique that is very popular among sales people is the "Noah's Ark" tactic, also known as "The Bandwagon Close." This gambit is based on the behavioral law, the "follower effect."

Example

A group of pedestrians is waiting at an intersection to cross the street. Despite the fact that there is currently no traffic, everybody is patiently waiting for the light to turn green. After awhile, one pedestrian decides not to wait any longer and crosses the street. Immediately, a second pedestrian follows his example. After him follow the remaining people. Nobody wants to remain a law abiding citizen, and wait for the light to turn green. The "follower effect" subconsciously compels everyone not to be left out, and to do as others do.

How does this apply to our negotiation strategies? If a sales person manages to convey to the potential buyer that everyone is buying this particular product, he or she might have a sale.

This tactic can be stretched one step farther: "These products are selling like hot cakes! I can't reorder them fast enough to satisfy the demand." This message hints to the customer that, besides the product's popularity, there is also a distinct factor of scarcity involved. Therefore it is not only wise to buy now, but also to buy more than just one.

This technique has been around for a long time, but has not lost a bit of it's effectiveness. Just be prepared to back up your claims if your counterpart is not convinced.

32. Silence

A very efficient counter to almost any tactic used on you, would be silence. Plain and simple silence has unusual and powerful effects. Whether you just made an offer and are now waiting for your counterpart's response, or your opponent just sprung an offer on you that you find absolutely unacceptable, silence can do the job.

It is part of human nature that "dead air" is very uncomfortable. If you sit back and wait, the other party will end up volunteering concessions. Remember this rule: The person who speaks first loses.

The best counter for such "silence tactics" is even more silence. Sometimes, however, this does not work as planned. In that case you can simply restate your last offer, or say: "This is the best I can do." If you have to break the silence, just be careful not to do it by making concessions. Don't let human nature trick you into saying something you will later regret.

VIII

NEGOTIATION POWER

For many people the word "power" carries a negative undertone. To become a successful negotiator, you have to understand that power is a perfectly ethical tool to influence other people. Power can be defined as the ability to influence people and in turn, control the outcome of a situation. Power itself is neither good nor bad — except when it is abused.

A critical element of power is rooted in everyone's state of mind. People with high self-esteem feel more powerful than people who have a low opinion of themselves. How much power do YOU have? The only way to really find out is to test it. Many of you will find that you are much more powerful than you think.

Power can be an attribute of interaction, or a reflection of certain conditions. It can be created in many ways, but power will exist only as long as it is accepted by all the people in the interaction. You need at least two people for a condition of power to exist.

Example

I was running late for a seminar in Las Vegas, Nevada. I could not believe the immense line for hotel check-in. Although several clerks were assisting the hotel guests, I could have waited at least twenty to thirty minutes. I then noticed a "VIP check-in" with only one person in line. I knew I was not a VIP guest in this hotel, but I got in the VIP line anyway.

A few moments later I was checked in without any problems. I eliminated the power of the "for VIP guests only" restriction, simply by not accepting it.

Negotiation power can be categorized into six source groups:

1. Title Power

Anyone in position of authority in a company probably has a business title, which gives him or her Title Power. This form of power is also referred to as Legitimate Power or Position Power.

I remember an interesting research project in which eighty candidates had to interview a business person. The same person was interviewed by all the candidates. Forty candidates were told that the gentleman they would interview was a mailroom supervisor. The other candidates were told that they would be interviewing the president of a Fortune 500 corporation.

After the interviews, each candidate filled out an evaluation sheet describing the interviewee. The candidates who thought they were interviewing the president, rated the person as much more powerful in the areas of knowledge, ability to influence, and authority than those who thought he worked in the mail room.

It is, therefore, absolutely advantageous to use Title Power whenever you can. Your business card, letterhead, name plate, etc. are good ways to express such power. It will certainly help influence people. At the same time, try not to be intimidated by anyone's title. Learn how to deal with Title Power.

2. Territorial Power

Try to arrange negotiations so that they are held on your own turf. Negotiating in your office puts you in a very advantageous position. For this very reason real estate agents make a point of using their own vehicles to drive clients when showing them homes.

These are more detailed tactics to enhance your Territorial Power:

♦ The chair that you sit in should be slightly higher than the chair of your opponent.

♦ Position yourself in front of a bright light source (like a large window), so that your negotiation partner is bound to look toward the light.

♦ You can have your secretary stage an incoming phone call from your opponent's competition to demonstrate, that there are other companies very interested in doing business with you.

I, however, advise caution when using these tactics. An experienced negotiator will have no problem detecting your power gambit from the start. This might create negative feelings about the way you conduct business, and it could cause more harm than good to your negotiations.

3. Reward and Punishment Power

Anyone in control of reward or punishment for you, has established another form of power.

Some personnel directors have absolute control over hiring, firing, raises, promotions, incentive bonuses, etc., so that their high amount of Reward and Punishment Power is not at all surprising.

One special form of Punishment Power is Embarrassment Power. The fear of embarrassment is so deeply rooted in the human psyche, that we sometimes find ourselves doing things we really don't want to do. We are driven solely by the fear of embarrassment.

Example

I used to organize sports promotions and special events. After an acrobatic and tumbling group finished its performance during a county fair, we had time left to roam around and enjoy ourselves. When some of the athletes and coaches of the show group discovered the highlight of the fair, a 180-foot bungee jump tower, they instantly tried to persuade me to take a plunge. When I stood in the little cage 180 feet off the ground, I realized I had only two options:

A)   I could ask to be brought down the same way I came up, which would have resulted in humiliation.

B)   I could jump, which would result in a sure near-death experience.

Needless to say, I chose option B and preferred death over embarrassment.

4. Power of Consistent Values

People who have a consistent set of values tend to be placed in a power position by other people. An example of such a value consistency would be the Pope. Regardless of the possible differences in opinions one might have with the Pope, the fact is that his values are likely to remain consistent throughout his tenure. People respect this consistency of values.

The other extreme would be Ross Perot, who changed his mind about running for the U.S. presidency more than once during the 1992 election campaign. This "flip-flop" tactic made him un-electable for many people who originally planned to vote for him.

To earn respect in negotiations, stick to your values. Your opponents might not necessarily agree with you, but at least they know where you stand. They will value that.

5. Expertise Power

Once you convey to people that you know more than they do, you have created expertise power. Sometimes you will find yourself negotiating with people who definitely have greater knowledge than you. That's when you have to rely on other negotiation tactics to compensate for your shortcomings.

Some people specialize in demonstrating their expertise power by using unique and impressive words in their negotiations. The best defense to such a tactic is plain disarmament: "I'm sorry, but what exactly do you mean by...," repeating one of the unknown, multi-syllable words. After halting the discussion a few times to ask for explanation, your counterpart's attempts to use expertise power will most likely be aborted. This, in turn, will put the control of the negotiations in your hands.

If you happen to be an experienced poker player, you might want to bluff your opponent. It is not always easy to differentiate real knowledge with apparent knowledge. This in turn leads to the question, whether or not your opponent's knowledge is in fact real or maybe just apparent.

6. Information Power

We already established the important role of gathering information. I recommend you divide the information you gather into two categories: special information and giveaway information.

Special information is pertinent, valuable data. It is the kind of information that is kept restricted to the president, the CEO, and top management. The average employee knows that such information exists, but does not know its actual contents. Withholding such information from employees reserves a form of power to management.

Creating power by withholding information is instinctively used by little children. We have all heard the children's phrase: "I know something you don't know!" The interesting part of this is that it is absolutely irrelevant, how significant this information really is. Even if the other person is bluffing and does not have any information, just the thought that he or she may know something important creates a power situation.

On the other hand, we can place ourselves in a power position by sharing some information with other people. This shows that you have information that could be helpful to other people (similar to Expertise Power), but you just let them sample your knowledge. The real information remains concealed for the moment.

IX

RED FLAG PHRASES

The best way to explain legitimizers and red flag phrases is "reading between the lines." Certain words and phrases, frequently used in conversations and negotiations can express the exact opposite of what was actually said.

Here is a short overview of such "Red Flag" Phrases and their interpretation:

When somebody starts a sentence with a phrase like "In my humble opinion ...," you know he or she is everything but humble. This is a person who thinks very highly of him or herself. Whether or not this high opinion is justified remains to be seen. You can gain advantage in your negotiations when you play on this person's ego: "Do you think you will be able to convince your company to place an order of that size?"

You will most likely learn of something totally new and unexpected, when somebody starts a sentence with one of these phrases:

"As you are aware ...";
"By the way ...";

"As you probably already know ...";
or "Before I forget ..."

Remember TV inspector Columbo. On the way out, after interviewing a murder suspect, he would invariably turn to ask one more question.

"And, by the way," he would say. The tactic often lead to the solution of the mystery and the arrest of the murderer.

Another phrase you should award a closer look is: "We can work out the details later." The person using it wants you to believe that the main issues have already been settled. In fact, you will find that there are still several unanswered areas in your negotiations.

Beware of the "Don't worry!" statement. People who use it are trying to relay a soothing message to you, when in fact you have good reason to be concerned.

Legitimizers are words that enhance or alter a certain message. Pay close attention when a person starts a sentence with legitimizers such as "Truthfully," "Frankly," or "Honestly." A real estate agent once said to me: "Frankly, I don't think my seller will accept this offer. Why don't you suggest to your buyer to reconsider the price?" The legitimizer "frankly" told me that our offer was in fact quite acceptable to the seller, and his agent was just trying to increase the price.

Words like "however" and "but" are considered **Erasers**, because they tend to void and erase what has previously been said.

Example

A potential buyer: "Your services seem to be very beneficial for a business like mine, but I think they are a little overpriced." In the first part of the sentence, the potential buyer shows interest in your services. Then follows the eraser "but," which reverses the buyer's attitude. This is made clear in the second part of the sentence, when the buyer rejects your service.

This technique is sometimes used intentionally, to demonstrate interest, and to keep the seller motivated to make certain concessions.

X

PERSONALITY STYLES

It is very important to educate yourself about differences in personality styles if you want to be a successful negotiator. It is very common for an agreement to be unreachable simply because the two parties cannot get along.

The differences in acting and reacting throughout the negotiation process often are misinterpreted as lack of willingness to compromise. But the real problems lie in the different personality styles. Understanding these styles not only helps to improve the results of business negotiations, but also improves all interpersonal relationships.

It is very rare to find a person whose character matches only one of the listed types. Most people are a blend of two or more of the following character styles:

Dictators

Dictators like to get to the point. One of their favorite mottos is: "Time is Money, and Money is Power!" So don't waste much time on small talk and idle chitchat with a person of this character. When presenting a proposal to a dictator, don't drown him or her in a report counting fifty pages or more. Highlight what you want him to read and affix stick-on notes on pages with essential contents. Dictators analyze a proposal on a purely logical level: "Is this investment going to yield satisfactory return?"

When dealing with this character type, do not make promises you cannot keep. The dictator will do anything to get the return that was promised, and usually takes complaints straight to the decision-making person at the top. As a matter of fact, they prefer to negotiate with powerful people.

People of this personality type always speak in a forthright, authoritative tone of voice. Their cold personalities have an extremely intimidating effect on others. That is why dictators are often feared. Dictators often have an extremely firm handshake that can crush a fragile hand.

Negotiating with this type of person can prove to be a rather demanding undertaking. Dictators make you feel that most things with them are not negotiable. The best way to break this barrier is to offer something to them in return. Dictators will become very interested in a negotiation process if they sense that there is something to be gained.

محايلات **Pluses:**
Assertive; organized; decisive; analytical; calculating.

Minuses:

Too much of a perfectionist; feels he is always right; intimidating; others can never meet the dictator's expectations.

Guerrillas

Guerrillas are very extroverted and social individuals. They enjoy being the center of attention, and they hope that all eyes will be upon them when they walk into a room. This outgoing personality is usually advertised by the way they dress.

Women like to wear bright colors and are not afraid to make a fashion statement. Men will either express their personality by wearing expensive designer suits or by a much more boisterous approach such as suspenders, cartoon ties, and dominating patterns on their jacket.

Guerrillas usually have trouble sitting or standing still. They are full of high energy and expect that others are always watching them out of admiration. This energy is used to achieve and maintain the dominating role in any situation. The guerrilla type is impatient and expects immediate attention.

They don't like to take prisoners and tend to go for the "kill." Once their prey has been wounded, they enjoy feasting, and seldom know when to stop. The most interesting aspect of guerrillas is, that underneath this vicious facade often hides a weak and fearful person.

Pluses:

Creative; ambitious; charismatic; competitive; strong social skills.

Minuses:
Sometimes untrustworthy; demeaning; conceded; vengeful.

Amiables

The amiable types are known for their smiles. They smile when they talk on the phone, ride in the elevator, or sit in a restaurant. This makes it somewhat difficult to identify how they really feel. But this pleasant personality type does not come without drawbacks:

If amiables are asked to voice their honest opinion about a matter, they will censor their answers to avoid hurt feelings. Because they want you to feel comfortable and happy, they may inquire anxiously about your needs and desires. They like to offer their help and assistance — mostly with a hidden agenda: They like others to be indebted. Another disadvantage of dealing with an amiable person is that it can take them a very long time to reach a decision.

Their body language includes many gestures of affection, such as embraces, arms around shoulders, etc. Their hand shakes are typically two-handed — the left hand over the top of yours or on your right elbow.

Pluses:
Very sociable; their agreeable attitude causes people to pour their heart out to them; good listeners.

Minuses:
Tend to use flattering remarks to manipulate people; frequently have a hidden agenda.

Silhouettes

When others kill with kindness, the silhouettes kill with silence — or at least they try to. They are usually not the most successful negotiators, but once in awhile their strategy of silence can score a home run.

When negotiating with silhouettes, be careful not to talk yourself into a corner. You will end up getting tangled in their web of silence.

Silhouettes like to save money and are often described as cheap. Be aware of the diversions that are frequently created by silhouettes.

People with this personality type prefer more personal space than others. They easily get uncomfortable and possibly claustrophobic when they find themselves in a very crowded environment.

Pluses:
Motivated; creative; modest; discrete; trustworthy; loyal.

Minuses:
Their silence makes them almost invisible. They are often overlooked. They are not assertive enough.

Appeasers

These character types are virtually helpless in any negotiation, as well as in many other everyday situations. Appeasers are afraid to take risks. They prefer to ask someone else to take care of unpleasant tasks. They try to avoid confrontations at any price.

Pluses:
Genuinely nice people; cheerful; helpful; loyal; appreciative.

Minuses:
Extremely insecure; unable to handle confrontations and conflicts; very indecisive, feel compelled to agree with others about everything.

It is possible to intentionally alter and modify your natural characteristics, but it requires hard work and a great amount of self-discipline. It is a fact that your behavior will have an effect on the people around you. If you manage to adapt all of the positive aspects, and eliminate your negative attributes, you have achieved the character style of a successful win-win negotiator.

The desirable characteristics of a win-win negotiator are:

- Not being afraid to assert yourself when necessary.
- Sticking to the facts without bragging to make a point.
- Focusing on solving a problem rather than creating one.

- Realizing that successful negotiating is based on a certain degree of collaboration with your counterpart.
- Not being afraid to walk away from a hopeless situation.
- Avoiding emotional involvement in the negotiation process.

XI

BODY LANGUAGE
The Language of Negotiators

This chapter presents an overview of nonverbal communication. Body language is a large and complex topic. Only the fundamentals that directly apply to the negotiation process are presented here. As in any other language, body language requires plenty of practice to be able to interpret and understand it accurately.

A good place to practice and study body language is an airport. Next time you are waiting for your boarding call, examine the non-verbal signals of other travellers. Observe people talking on the phone: Are they talking to their boss, their client, their spouse, their boy or girl friend? With a little practice you will be able to read their body language quite well.

It is very important to stress that a single sign or gesture is often not conclusive enough to indicate a certain feeling or behavior. Just like a single word can seldom express feelings or facts to the same extent that an entire sentence can. It is important to look for other signals. If all nonverbal messages support each other, a more conclusive picture has been drawn. We consider this a matching cluster.

Also be aware that changes of body language are an especially valid indicator. A witness in court who frequently scratches his nose could give the impression that he is lying, but might in fact just have an itchy nose. However, if during the line of questioning his hand is brought up to the side of his nose, this could very well be an indication that he is not telling the truth.

Example

A person crossing his arms in front of his chest generally conveys disagreement. But if he also slides to the very front edge of his chair and rocks his feet forward to tiptoe, he is sending signs of cooperation and acceptance. To focus solely on the arm position and to assume disapproval on that basis, would therefore be premature and incorrect. A simple explanation for the crossed arms may be that your counterpart is cold.

The best way to read a person is to look for consistency between their verbal and nonverbal communications, and for changing expressions. If somebody tells you that he really likes your ideas, but his body language expresses resentment or suspicion, you will doubt the person's honesty due to the inconsistency of words and gestures.

On the other hand, if verbal and nonverbal communication signals match, you have reason to believe the person is truthful with you. Always try to separate verbal statements and nonverbal signs. This will help you in everyday judgements of business, as well as social contacts.

Experienced negotiators will be able to control the body language signals they send. Their signs of confidence and openness might be nothing but a cover-up. The non-verbal signals sent during the first thirty seconds of a negotiation are the most reflective of your counterpart's true posture.

While you listen to your counterpart and attempt to interpret his or her body language, your own nonverbal signals may be under scrutiny. Periodically "check in" on anything you might be subconsciously doing with your own body.

The following outline of gestures and body positions and their interpretation will be a helpful guide during negotiations:

Eye Contact

During face to face communications it is very important to put emphasis on every form of eye contact. People who shy away from looking at their conversation partners while talking to them are perceived as dishonest. It signals that they have something to hide or are not telling the truth. This is true in most cases, but psychologists know that avoiding eye contact can also be caused by insecurity. Either way, if your negotiation counterpart cannot maintain eye contact with you, you can bet that nothing good will result from these negotiations. It is easier for some people to maintain eye contact while they are listening than while they are talking.

The way people blink can tell us something about them. Rapid blinking often accompanies statements that are not true. However, be aware that some people may suffer from a nervous disorder that increases their blink frequency.

Arms Crossed

Crossed arms generally signal a defensive posture. The best way to get your opponent out of the defensive mode, is to relate to him or her. It is important that your counterpart not feel threatened by you. A person who feels uneasy during a negotiation will withdraw from the communication process, harming any chance of reaching an agreement.

There is a possibility that a person has his arms crossed solely for reasons of comfort. A look at the person's hands will help shed some light on the real reason. If the hands hold tightly to the arms, it definitely signals a defensive posture.

Legs Crossed

Crossed legs can also signal a protective attitude. Watch out for a person with arms and legs crossed. These two elements are enough evidence to be interpreted as a strong adversary cluster. Negotiations in which neither party has his legs crossed usually have a much greater potential to be successful.

Locked Ankles

Sitting with locked ankles signals apprehension, especially if the locked ankles are accompanied by hands clenched on the arms of a chair or to each other. A person sitting in this manner is holding something back. This could either be pertinent information, or true feelings and thoughts regarding a specific matter.

Showing the Palms of the Hands

Hands and hand positions have always played an important role in negotiations. The hand shake originated as a symbol of peace. People who shake hands prove that they aren't holding a weapon. Showing the palms of the hands during a conversation symbolizes openness and sincerity.

Hands in Pocket

People who hide their hands in their pockets show insecurity. Very often they are not quite open and are holding something back, especially when they bury their hands entirely, including their thumbs.

Hands on Hips

Someone who stands with his hands on his hips indicates readiness to become involved in a conversation. It expresses willingness to become an active part of the event. Very often this signal is accompanied by a wider stance.

Hands Steepled

When the fingertips of both hands are brought together and resemble the shape of a church steeple, it signifies a great amount of self-confidence. It is the gesture of people who are very sure of themselves.

Drumming and Tapping

Drumming fingers indicate boredom, particularly when accompanied by any form of tapping or twitching with one or both feet. If you find these signs in your counterpart during a negotiation, it is essential to stimulate interest, or the negotiations will stall.

Tilted Head

The position of the head can reveal how much attention is being paid. A listener whose head is in a straight upright position may not be very attentive. A person who listens with his head slightly tilted to one side, is paying much more attention, especially if this is accompanied by the hand being put up to the chin.

Hand on the Back of the Neck

Beware if your counterpart moves his hand to the back of his neck. Whether he is loosening his collar, or holding or rubbing the back of his neck, he is annoyed and maybe even angry about something you just said. What this gesture should tell you is that you are a "pain in the neck," and you better change your negotiation strategy.

Tugging on Ear

Rubbing the earlobe or tugging slightly on the ear are signs that a person is interested in what you have to say, and that he or she wants to hear more about it. A similar message is sent by putting the end of a pen or the ear piece of a pair of glasses to or into the mouth.

Body Shifting

If your counterpart shifts his entire body so that his feet are pointing toward the exit, he is signaling his wish to end the conversation. This can also be observed at social gatherings. The host keeps talking and the guest is positioning his body as if to leave. In negotiations, it is impossible to convince the other party once they have signaled that they want to end the negotiations.

Don't Underestimate Non-verbal Power

During a negotiation, most messages are conveyed by body language, not verbally. This finding emphasizes the importance of proper understanding of non-verbal behavior. Knowing the basics of body language will help you in many ways.

1.   It will help you to understand the true feelings of your counterparts. In negotiation it is invaluable to know where your opponents stand, and if they are telling the

truth. By their reactions you can see what impact each factor of your presentation has.

2.   By intentionally sending body language signals to your opponents, you can sometimes bluff effectively. Even if your counterparts have no knowledge of body language, their subconscious will be able to perceive these non-verbal messages. It is therefore important, to select and use gesture clusters wisely in order to paint the picture of your choice.

These two aspects are widely understood. Experts agree on their important impact in our lives. When body language signals are sent intentionally, they have a two-way effect. It not only portrays a certain attitude to your counterpart, it influences you to adopt that attitude.

Example

To signal self-confidence and openness, uncross your legs, place your feet flat on the ground, steeple your fingers, and maintain good eye contact. This cluster of gestures will persuade your opponent that you are confident, dominant, and open. In addition, it will boost your own self-confidence. You will feel in charge, your confidence level will be high, and you will have no problem with being open to your counterpart.

XII

THE BOTTOM LINE

You negotiate throughout your life. On a professional level, when you are dealing with other businesses, vendors, and clients, or when you are discussing a raise. On a personal level, when presenting a complaint to the customer service department, or when buying a new car. To increase your odds of getting what you want, you must apply appropriate negotiation techniques.

In simple, everyday situations, you will get by with using only one or two basic negotiation tactics. However, for more complex negotiation issues, you need a more sophisticated arsenal of gambits to do the trick:

Preliminary Steps

Do your homework. Find out what the other party actually wants, and if there is a way for you to make that possible. Learn what your counterparts' motivation is. How eager is he or she to sell or buy? Does the other party want to rush to a solution?

The First Offer

Let the other party make the first offer. This puts you in a better position for further negotiations. Once your counterpart has presented you with the first offer, it is unwise to accept it right away. By accepting the first offer, you are forfeiting any possible gain through negotiating.

Basic Rules

Don't paint yourself into a corner by narrowing a negotiation down to only one issue. There is always more than one issue that can become a vital part of the negotiation process.

Remember, people usually don't want the same things. Issues that are very important for me might be much less important to you.

Know your final price. If you are negotiating the purchase of goods or services, you should know the maximum price you are willing to pay, prior to entering the negotiations. If you are on the seller's side, establish the lowest price at which you are willing to sell. Any decent negotiator enters a negotiation only after setting this "secret number."

Gather Information

The main focus of doing your homework, however, will be to gather information about the other side. The more you know about your counterpart, the better your chances of success will become. The party who has more information will be in control, and the party in control will find it easier to achieve success in negotiations. A very important factor in the quest for gathering information is to listen. The more you get the other parties to talk about their needs and wants, the smoother the negotiation phase will be.

Do not interrupt them. Remember that by interrupting you might miss a vital piece of information.

Always control your emotions! If you get upset, you will give away your controlling position. Getting angry hinders your ability to think logically, and it will significantly impair your problem-solving ability.

Walk Away Power

The worst thing that can happen to you during a negotiation is that your opponent realizes that you are determined to close the deal at any cost. It is essential that you never rule out the option to walk away from a negotiation, if you don't feel comfortable with the terms.

Demonstrating walk away power will give you significant leverage throughout your negotiations. Remember: *The person who wants it least, wins.*

Practice Negotiation Tactics

Always bare in mind that negotiating pressure always affects both parties equally. Practicing the negotiation gambits from this book, will increase your confidence and, in turn, your success. Start practicing with trivial, everyday situations, and move on to more complex tactics as you get better.

One of the basic negotiation techniques is the *Higher Authority Method*, which can be very effectively combined with the *Good Guy-Bad Guy* tactic.

The most efficient way to implement the Higher Authority method is to employ a vague entity. Committees, board of directors, or commissions are ideal. This technique is popular because one can put pressure on the other party without assuming the role of the confrontational "bad guy."

It will make your negotiations much easier if you know what your opponent's bottom-line figure is. You can find out what the other party's "secret number" is by sending a *Trial Balloon*.

Unless you are negotiating with a company that holds an absolute monopoly position with a specific product, you will always find a competitor who sells a comparable, if not identical product. Use this element in your negotiations by applying the *Competition Gambit*. You can also create such a situation by bluffing. Unless your counterpart really knows the market well enough to call your bluff, you will probably get away with it.

Don't underestimate the power of the written word. *The Written Advantage* can easily be incorporated in your negotiations tactics. The written word will be questioned much less frequently than the spoken word.

Become the party in charge of preparing the final contract. There will always be some details that have not been finalized during the negotiations, which you can interpret to be more favorable to you. Very often your counterpart will simply agree with the contract and sign it in its original form. This tactic is referred to as *"Fait accompli."*

Always *ask for more* than you are willing to settle for. This is to keep your adversary busy wrestling with your unreasonable proposal, and to give you the space to confer a feeling of satisfaction to the opposing party by reducing your original proposal.

Beware of *Time Pressure*! The person who has to negotiate under time pressure has a disadvantage. Skilled negotiators often manage to create a scenario where the other party is facing serious time pressure. You should realize that almost every deadline can be changed or extended.

Stay calm and patient when you are negotiating. It is unlikely that you will achieve the best possible outcome if you rush it. Remember the *Pareto principle*: Eighty percent of the negotiated agreements transpire in the last twenty percent of the time spent negotiating.

Negotiation Power

Anyone who holds a leading position with a business title, possesses *Title Power*. It is advantageous to use *Title Power* whenever you can. Your business card, letterhead, name plate, etc. are good ways to express such power. It will certainly help influence people. At the same time you should not be intimidated by somebody else's title.

Use your *Territorial Power* by arranging negotiations to be held on your own home turf.

A possible lack of Title Power, Expertise Power, or Territorial Power can be compensated by boosting your *Information Power*. You can place yourself in a power position by sharing some information with other people. This shows that you have information that could be helpful to other people (similar to Expertise Power). However, let them only sample your knowledge, and keep the real information remains concealed for the moment.

Reading Between the Lines

In order to become a successful negotiator, you have to learn to identify and interpret *red flag phrases*.

Legitimizers are words that enhance or alter a message. Some of the most common *legitimizers* are "truthfully," "frankly," and "honestly."

Words like "however" and "but" are considered *erasers*, because they tend to void and erase what was previously said.

Personality Types

Part of studying your opponents is to understand their personality types. Most people are a blend of two or more character styles. Understanding personality styles not only helps you improve the results of business negotiations, but will also better your ability to interact in all interpersonal relationships.

Dictators like to get to the point. One of their favorite mottos is: "Time is Money, and Money is Power!" Their cold personalities have an extremely intimidating effect on others. Dictators are often feared.

Guerrillas are very extroverted and socially active individuals. They enjoy being the center of attention. The guerrilla type is impatient and expects immediate attention.

Amiables will censor what they say to avoid hurt feelings. They like to offer their help and assistance, often to the point of annoyance.

While others might kill with kindness, *Silhouettes* kill with silence. They are usually not the most successful negotiators, but once in a while their strategy of silence can score a home run. They may feel uncomfortable when they find themselves in a crowded environment.

Appeasers are not only helpless in negotiations, but also in many other everyday situations. They are afraid to take risks, and try to avoid confrontations at any price.

Body Language

Body language is complex and requires plenty of practice to be interpreted and understood accurately.

A single sign or gesture is often not conclusive enough to indicate a certain feeling or behavior. It is therefore important to look for other, matching signals. Changes of body language can also be perceived as valid indicators.

Experienced negotiators will be able to control the body language signals they are sending your way. Their signs of confidence and openness may be either genuine or nothing but an effective cover-up. Non-verbal signals sent during the first thirty seconds of a negotiation most accurately reflect the true posture of the sender.

While you are analyzing your opponent's body language, your own nonverbal signals should be observed. "Check in" periodically with anything you might be subconsciously doing with your own body.

XIII

AFTERWORD

Always remember to aim for WIN-WIN outcomes!

On that note, I hope that this book has provided you with useful insight into negotiation processes. Now, put your negotiation knowledge to the test. Good luck!

BIBLIOGRAPHY

Dawson, Roger. *You Can Get Anything You Want.* Phoenix, AZ: Regency Books, Inc., 1985

Kurth, Hanns. *Menschenkenntnis auf den ersten Blick.* Landsberg am Lech, Germany: Moderne Verlags Gesellschaft Mbh, 1984

McCormack, Mark. *What They Don't Teach You at Harvard Business School.* New York, NY: Bantam Books, 1984

Nierenberg, Gerald I. and Calero, Henry H. *How to Read a Person Like a Book.* New York, NY: Pocket Books, 1971

Schapiro, Nicole. *Negotiating for Your Life.* New York, NY: Henry Holt and Company, Inc., 1993

Shenson, Howard L. and Wilson, Jerry R. *138 Quick Ideas to Get More Clients.* New York, NY: John Wiley & Sons, Inc., 1993

Stark, Peter B. *It's Negotiable.* San Diego, CA: Pfeiffer & Company, 1994

About the Author:

Mike R. Stark is an international marketing and management consultant. He also teaches workshops and seminars in negotiation, marketing, and management matters. Mike Stark is available for keynote speeches and workshops. For further information contact:

> Trimark Publishing
> Author Department
> 5035 S. Kipling B-3, Suite 109
> Littleton, CO 80127

INDEX